The Angela T.

The 400th Year Commemoration Ceremony
1619-2019: Commemorating 400 Years of Institutionalized Slavery in Colonized America

Copyright © 2019
Revised Edition 2020

Written by Cheri L. Mills for Simmons College of Kentucky
Edited by Olivia M. Cloud
Cover Design by Tyler Anderson

ISBN: 978-0-9785572-9-4

All proceeds benefit the advancement of Simmons College of Kentucky, the nation's 107th HBCU.

Simmons College of Kentucky
1000 South 4th Street
Louisville, Kentucky 40203
502.776.1443
www.simmonscollegeky.edu

**THE ANGELA PROJECT
LIBERATION CEREMONY**
is named to commemorate the first African to arrive in the American Colonies for the purpose of enslavement.

Share your experience!

#WeAreAngela400SCKY

Song

The Black National Anthem (Lift Every Voice and Sing)
Written by James Weldon Johnson (1900)
Composed by John Rosamond Johnson (1905)

Verse 1

Lift ev'ry voice and sing,
Till earth and heaven ring.
Ring with the harmonies of Liberty;
Let our rejoicing rise,
High as the list'ning skies,
Let it resound loud as the rolling sea.
Sing a song full of the faith that the dark past has taught us,
Sing a song full of the hope that the present has brought us;
Facing the rising sun of our new day begun,
Let us march on till victory is won.

Slavery Era
(1619 – 1865)

WHITES *(Leaders and People):* On behalf of Europe and the Western World, we repent for the enslavement of black people. We repent for kidnapping you from your native land of Africa, putting you in chains, and under the brutality of the whip, forcing you to lie down, chained together in the dark, damp bottom of cargo ships for months, where millions of you died as we transported you to America to be exploited as free labor in the cotton fields that built white wealth.

We repent for whipping you into states of physical and mental unconsciousness. We repent for the physical scars inflicted when we beat your naked backs until they were bloodied and permanently scarred. We repent for the emotional scars inflicted as we denigrated your human worth and discredited your value.

We repent for raping your mothers, and for violating your daughters who were yet children and robbing them of innocence. We repent for treating you like cattle and regarding you as animals—tearing your families apart and auctioning off your relations—separating mothers from fathers, and sisters from brothers and children from parents—to reap payment from the highest bidder.

We denounce the deafening of our ears to your piercing cries for mercy and the hardening of our hearts against compassion for your plight. We lament our vicious retaliation for the times when you followed the innate human desire for freedom: we lynched your bodies and left them to rot in the trees; we amputated and humiliated you to disconnect you from feelings of wholeness. We snatched up your mothers, fathers, sisters and brothers, hung them by their ankles, and burned them alive simply to protect and preserve the perverse institution of slavery.

O Lord, have mercy! We repent of our intergenerational acceptance of vitriol and disregard toward our black brothers and sisters, which has manifested as racism and discrimination. We rebuke our acquiescence through our participation and our culpability through our silence. We repent and seek your forgiveness.

● ● ● ● ● ●

BLACKS (Leaders and People): On behalf of black people, we forgive you. We repent of the hatred and unforgiveness that we have harbored toward you for the enslavement of black people and for injurious actions that you inflicted upon us through multiple generations.

We forgive you for kidnapping us from our native land of Africa, putting us in chains, and under the scourge of the whip, forcing us to lie down chained together in the dark, damp and unsanitary bottom of ships for months, where millions of our forbears died, as you transported free labor to America to work your cotton fields to build the white wealth which still profits you today.

We forgive you for whipping us into states of physical and mental unconsciousness. We forgive you for the physical scars inflicted when you beat our naked backs until they were bloodied and permanently scarred. We forgive you for the emotional scars inflicted as you denigrated our human worth and discredited our value. We forgive you for raping our mothers, and for violating our daughters who were yet children and robbing them of innocence.

We forgive you for treating us like cattle and regarding us as animals—tearing our families apart and auctioning off our relations—separating mothers from fathers, and sisters from brothers and children from parents—to reap payment from the highest bidder. We denounce the deafening of your ears to our piercing cries for mercy and the hardening of your hearts against compassion for our plight. We release the pain of your vicious retaliation for the times when we followed the innate human desire for freedom: you lynched our bodies and left them to rot in the trees; you amputated and humiliated us to disconnect us from feelings of wholeness. You snatched up our mothers, fathers, sisters and brothers, hung them by their ankles, and burned them alive simply to protect and preserve the perverse institution of slavery.

O Lord, have mercy! We forgive your intergenerational acceptance of vitriol and disregard toward our people, which has manifested as racism and discrimination. We forgive your acquiescence through your participation and your culpability through your silence. We forgive and strive to move forward, governed by the mercy of Almighty God who, in Christ Jesus, forgives all sin.

Song

The Black National Anthem (Lift Every Voice and Sing)
Written by James Weldon Johnson (1900)
Composed by John Rosamond Johnson (1905)

Verse 2
Stony the road we trod,
Bitter the chast'ning rod,
Felt in the days when hope unborn had died;
Yet with a steady beat,
Have not our weary feet,
Come to the place for which our fathers sighed?
We have come over a way that with tears has been watered,
We have come, treading our path through
the blood of the slaughtered,
Out from the gloomy past,
Here now we stand at last
Where the white gleam of our bright star is cast.

Jim Crow Era
(1877 – 1969)

WHITES *(Leaders and People)*: On behalf of Europe and the Western World, we repent of the repeal of Field Order 15, which deprived black families of their promised 40 acres and a mule. We repent for post-slavery sabotage and neglect that plummeted blacks from enslavement to deprivation—leaving you with no education, food, money, land, advocates, so that blacks were forced to return to plantations as *de facto* slaves. We repent for Confederates who rebelled against the United States had their land and power restored, while blacks who loyally fought to save the Union were deprived.

We repent for strategically restricting black aspiration to menial, low-wage jobs that secured your negative economic plight. We repent for the exploitation of black labor through sharecropping.

We repent for violently depriving blacks of their voting rights, of the right to serve on juries, and the right to political representation, despite your equal taxation. We repent for the retaliatory lynchings and terrorism that caused black people to live in fear as you fought for your basic rights as Americans.

We repent of the race riots, such as those levied on Tulsa's Black Wall Street and in other communities, devastating their black economic base. We repent for the demeaning depiction of black image as buffoons in cinema and advertisement. We repent for the Eugenics Movement, which sought to eliminate blackness, and other traits deemed inferior, through birth control and abortion.

We repent for crafting the theological rationalization of black inferiority and dehumanization. We repent for the sin of omission for refusing to speak against a system brutalizing blackness. We repent for our endorsement of this cruel and inhumane treatment of our black brothers and sisters through our participation and through our silence and through our perpetuation, and we seek your forgiveness and seek to move forward in agape.

• • • • • •

BLACKS *(Leaders and People)*: On behalf of all black people, we forgive you.

We forgive your post-slavery sabotage and neglect that plummeted black people from enslavement to deprivation—leaving us with no education, food, money, land, advocates, so that blacks were forced to return to plantations as *de facto* slaves. We forgive you for upholding Confederates who rebelled against the United States having their land and power restored, while blacks who loyally fought to save the Union were deprived.

We forgive your strategic restriction of black aspiration to menial, low-wage jobs that secured our negative economic plight. We forgive you for the exploitation of black labor through sharecropping.

We forgive you for violently depriving blacks of their voting rights, of the right to serve on juries, and the right to political representation, despite our equal taxation. We forgive you for the retaliatory lynchings and terrorism that caused black people to live in fear as we fought for our basic rights as Americans.

We forgive you for the race riots, such as those levied on Tulsa's Black Wall Street and in other communities, devastating their black economic base. We forgive you for the demeaning depiction of black image as buffoons in cinema and advertisement. We pardon the Eugenics Movement, which sought to eliminate blackness, and other traits deemed inferior, through birth control and abortion.

We forgive you for crafting the theological rationalization of black inferiority and dehumanization. We forgive your sin of omission for refusing to speak against a system brutalizing blackness. We forgive your endorsement of this cruel and inhumane treatment of our black people through your participation and through your silence and through your perpetuation, and we harbor neither anger nor resentment as we move forward in agape.

Song
The Black National Anthem (Lift Every Voice and Sing)
Written by James Weldon Johnson (1900)
Composed by John Rosamond Johnson (1905)

Verse 3
God of our weary years,
God of our silent tears,
Thou who has brought us thus far on the way;

Thou who has by Thy might,
Led us into the light,
Keep us forever in the path, we pray.
Lest our feet stray from the places, our God, where we met Thee,
Lest our hearts, drunk with the wine of the world, we forgot Thee,
Shadowed beneath thy hand,
May we forever stand,
True to our God,
True to our native land.

The Aftereffects
1970 – The Present Day

WHITES *(Leaders and People):* On behalf of Europe and the Western World, we repent for disinvestment in the black community, whereby redlining is widely practiced, with banks and insurance companies refusing to do business in black areas. We repent for the consequence of underdevelopment in black areas, resulting in impoverished black communities across the United States of America. We repent for, by intent or neglect, allowing ghettoization. When blacks moved in, whites moved out, along with the employment opportunities. Before the jobs left the cities to go to other countries, they first flocked to the suburbs with fleeing whites.

We repent for leaving blacks in isolated communities, unable to relocate to parcels of opportunity because of restrictive covenants. We repent for the redlined communities where blacks were stuck and left to the mercy of slumlords because you could not get bank loans to own your own houses and businesses.

We repent for the mass incarceration of black men—for there are more black men incarcerated in America than the prison populations of India, Argentina, Canada, Lebanon, Japan, Germany, Finland, Israel and England combined. From a total population of two billion in nine countries, they have 742,000 behind bars. In America, 745,000 black men are behind bars. Black people are 13 percent of the population, but control only 2 percent of the nation's wealth and comprise 40 percent of the US prison population.

We repent for our endorsement of this recklessly brutal treatment of our black brothers and sisters through our participation and through our silence, and we ask your forgiveness.

• • • • • •

BLACKS *(Leaders and People):* On behalf of black people, we forgive you. We repent of the hatred and unforgiveness that we have held toward the white race for your disinvestment in the black community, whereby redlining is widely practiced, with banks and insurance companies refusing to do business in black areas. We forgive you for allowing the consequences of underdevelopment in black areas, resulting in impoverished black communities across the United States of America. We forgive you for, by intent or neglect, allowing ghettoization. When blacks moved in, whites moved out, along with the employment opportunities. Before the jobs left the cities to go to other countries, they first flocked to the suburbs with fleeing whites.

We forgive you for leaving blacks in isolated communities, unable to relocate to parcels of opportunity because of restrictive covenants. We forgive you for designing redlined communities where blacks were stuck and left to the mercy of slumlords because we could not get bank loans to own houses and businesses.

We forgive you for the mass incarceration of black men—for there are more black men incarcerated in America than the prison populations of India, Argentina, Canada, Lebanon, Japan, Germany, Finland, Israel and England combined. From a total population of two billion in nine countries, they have 742,000 behind bars. In America, 745,000 black men are behind bars. black people are 13 percent of the population, but control only 2 percent of the nation's wealth and comprise 40 percent of the US prison population.

We forgive you for your endorsement of this recklessly brutal treatment of us, your black brothers and sisters, through your participation and through your silence, and offer our unfettered forgiveness.

Song
The Battle Hymn of the Republic
Lyrics by Julia Ward Howe (1861)

Verse 1
Mine eyes have seen the glory of the coming of the Lord;
He is trampling out the vintage
where the grapes of wrath are stored:
He hath loosed the fateful lightning of His terrible swift sword,
His truth is marching on.

Chorus
Glory, Glory, Hallelujah! Glory, Glory Hallelujah!
Glory, Glory, Hallelujah! His truth is marching on.

Our Call to God for Help

"Do this and the lights will turn on, and your lives will turn around at once. Your righteousness will pave your way. The God of glory will secure your passage. Then when you pray, God will answer. You'll call out for help and I'll say, 'Here I am.'" Isaiah 58:8

ALL: Lord, we have humbled ourselves before You in fasting and prayer. You said in Isaiah 58 to do this and the lights would turn on, and that our lives would turn around at once. You also said that when we pray, You will answer. And that when we call out for help, You will say, "Here I am."

Lord, on behalf of black people everywhere, we call out to You for help. Lord, we beseech you:

MEN: We ask that black people will no longer bear the societal burden and emotional scars of centuries of enslavement, America's national shame.

WOMEN: O Lord, Heal Our Land.

We ask that there will be an acknowledgment of America's original sin.

MEN: Heal our land, O Lord.

We ask that HBCU's will be endowed in perpetuity, for the perpetuation of black education.

WOMEN: O Lord, heal our land.

We ask that there be more investments in black education through black institutions.

MEN: Heal our land, O Lord.

We ask that Black America would be designated as America's indebted people, and that reparations be provided to reflect this status.

WOMEN: O Lord, heal our land.

We ask that You restore the five black pillar institutions: The Black Church, the black family, black schools, black businesses and black media.

WOMEN: Heal our land, O Lord.

We ask that there will be reformed policing, based on crime and not color.

MEN: O Lord, heal our land.

We ask that You end the inequities of mass incarceration that has contributed to the crippling of black families and black communities.

WOMEN: Heal our land, O Lord.

We ask that You free victims of the Clinton crime bill that has especially robbed communities of black men.

MEN: O Lord, heal our land.

We ask for the reform of collegiate sports, to focus on education and not exploitation."

WOMEN: Heal our land, O Lord.

We ask that government will subsidize college tuition rather than corporate greed.

MEN: O Lord, heal our land.

We ask that there will be no-interest business loans.

WOMEN: O Lord, heal our Land.

MEN: Heal our land, O Lord.

ALL: Now to the One who is able to do immeasurably more than all we ask or imagine, according to divine power that is at work within us, to God be glory in the church and in Christ Jesus throughout all generations, for ever and ever! In Jesus Name. Amen.

Song
The Battle Hymn of the Republic (Chorus)
Lyrics by Julia Ward Howe (1861)

Chorus
Glory, Glory, Hallelujah! Glory, Glory Hallelujah!
Glory, Glory, Hallelujah! His truth is marching on.

Closing Declaration
"We are the Voice of One"

Prayer Declaration*
We are the Voice of One that crieth in [your city/state]:
"Prepare Ye the way of the Lord!
Make straight in [your city/state], a highway for our God
Every valley in [your city/state] shall be exalted
And every mountain and hill in [your city/state]
  shall be brought low.
The crooked places in [your city/state] shall be made straight
And the rough places shall be made smooth
And the glory of the Lord shall be revealed in [your city/state]
And all of [your city/state] and all nations shall see it together
for the mouth of the Lord has spoken it!"

Heavenly Father, make us one,
just as You and the Lord Jesus are One!
Heavenly Father, increase our numbers
and gather Your people to pray!
Let the Holy Spirit move freely,
and the zeal of the Lord of Hosts shall accomplish it!
In Jesus' name! Amen!

Song
The Battle Hymn of the Republic
Lyrics by Julia Ward Howe (1861)

Verse 3
He has sounded forth the trumpet that shall never call retreat;
He is sifting out the hearts of men before His Judgment Seat.
Oh! Be swift, my soul, to answer Him, be jubilant, my feet!
Our God is marching on.

Chorus
Glory, Glory, Hallelujah! Glory, Glory Hallelujah!
Glory, Glory, Hallelujah! His truth is marching on.

* "We are the Voice of One" Prayer Declaration is adapted from Isaiah 40

"We will have to repent in this generation, not merely for the hateful words and actions of the bad people, but for the appalling silence of the good people. Human progress never rolls in on wheels of inevitability; it comes through the tireless efforts of men willing to be co-workers with God, and without this hard work, time itself becomes an ally of the forces of social stagnation. We must use time creatively, in the knowledge that the time is always ripe to do right."

– Dr. Martin Luther King, Jr.

Take Action!

Be a vocal advocate and support reparations for American Descendants of Slavery (ADOS). Contact your congressional and senate representatives today.

Support The Black Agenda for the American Descendants of Slavery. You may access The Black Agenda at *www.ados101.com*.

Advocate for the abolishment of unjust racial policies, laws, and practices at the local, state, and federal levels.

CPSIA information can be obtained
at www.ICGtesting.com
Printed in the USA
LVHW020044010820
662083LV00008B/486